György Kapocsy

THE HUNGARIAN PUSZTA

Kiskunság
Hortobágy

Corvina

Let us… go, riding full speed, toward the east where a magnificent sight appears, the Hortobágy!
Hortobágy, glorious plains, you are the brow of God. … How much farther the sun travels here than elsewhere! The horizon is limitless; it is like a round table covered with the glass jar of a light blue sky, undimmed by the tiniest cloud. It is a gorgeous spring day.
…The primeval silence sits musing on this spacious land…
Sándor Petőfi: Úti levelek Kerényi Frigyeshez [Letters to Frigyes Kerényi], 1847

The Hungarian Plain can be divided into three regions: Apaj, Bugac and Hortobágy. There one can still find the soothing atmosphere of tranquillity that derives from a landscape that stretches, monotonous and seemingly featureless, to the distant horizon. But we have only to examine the earth on which we stand to find that there is much of interest in this area. Where the pools have run dry, cracked earth has a surface of white alkaline substances which create a natural arrangement of pleasing forms. Here the sophisticated city dweller must adjust his expectations to the simple beauty and subtle atmosphere of the great plain, otherwise he may pass by without experiencing the fascination of these "empty" tracks of eastern Hungary.

The puszta has its own majesty, a visible reminder of the greater majesty of the entire universe, and a reminder that we ourselves are but as a grain of sand in the vastness of Infinity. "The primeval silence sits musing on this spacious land"—wrote Sándor Petőfi, the greatest poet of the Plain. But the history of the puszta is full of incident.

When the first Magyar settlers arrived in the last years of the 9th century these regions were partly wooded; elsewhere there were marshes, impenetrable pools, banks of reeds and an expanse of moorland. We have documentary evidence of more than 50

<<1. The puszta in winter

<2. Before the storm—stud farm in the Hortobágy

3. "The horizon is limitless, it is like a round table covered with the glass jar of a light blue sky…"

4. Petőfi's commemorative tree, struck by lightning, still standing in Dömsöd

5. In this wind-blown saline soil every plant struggles for life; so does the love grass

settlements in the Hortobágy, twelve of them with churches. There are also records of the monastery of Ohat and the abbey of Zám. Of these buildings there now remain only a few ruined walls.

Most of the ancient forests and settlements were destroyed in the 13th century. In 1241 the Mongols, led by Batu Khan, invaded Hungary from three directions and in April of that year the Hungarian army suffered a crushing defeat at Muhi. The Mongols, superior in numbers, drove all before them, burning the forests and destroying the villages. The Hungarian people sought refuge in walled towns, on islands and in the ridges of high ground surrounded by swamps and marshes through which no stranger could find a path. But even the churches could not provide asylum. When in the late 19th century the ruins of a church were excavated in the sandy area of Bugacmonostor, the archaeologists saw history come to life: there they found the huddled bones of those who had been crushed by the roof of the church as it crashed in flames.

Villages were abandoned and the landscape became a desert. We know nothing of the inhabitants except a few names which occur in contemporary records or which have been passed down from father to son. The medieval plagues also took their toll of the village people.

6. In Europe there are now fewer storks than formerly but on the Hungarian Plain in the National Parks of Hortobágy and Kiskunság they are to be found in increasing numbers

7. The livestock are still driven out to the pastures around the farmsteads

8. The setting sun marks the end of the day once timed by the lighting of shepherds' fires

The few who survived returned and attempted to rebuild their homes. They cut down more trees for building and heating and so the areas of forest were further diminished. For nearly two hundred years people struggled to survive, until the arrival of the Turks. In István Györffy's "Chronicle of the Nagykunság" he describes how "the final destruction of the Nagykunság came in 1683 when the Turks advanced with the intention of taking Vienna. The Mongol khan, Murad Giraj, ordered to join the sultan's main army, did so in 1683 by way of first Debrecen then Nagykunság."

And of the events of 1691 he wrote: "This time the threat came from the direction of Várad from which place the elder son of the Mongol khan, Sultan Gelga, set out to devastate the Plain with an army of 80,000 Turkish and Mongol soldiers. ... The local people were surrounded and hundreds of villages were burnt to the ground from Várad and Debrecen to the Tisza."

From these chronicles we know the fate of those who once inhabited the Hungarian Plain.

There remained the land. But even after the expulsion of the Turks, when there was a period of intensive cultivation and livestock-breeding, the desctruction of the landscape continued. In the middle of the 19th century the marshes were drained and the flow of the rivers, particularly that of the Tisza, was controlled. There was no more annual flooding of the land and therefore no more fertilizing sludge was deposited on the fields. The water plane was much reduced and in these new conditions the sodium salts rose to the surface and

9. Fires started as a consequence of spontaneous combustion or human carelessness can destroy vast areas before the people of the puszta can get them under control

10. It should not be thought that small farmers have an easy life; however, they do their best to bring gaiety into their lives

11. "The bells of a hundred fat cattle in Kiskunság resound under a dazzling sky..." (Sándor Petőfi: Az Alföld [The Plain])

caused alkalization. Meantime stud farms had been established and the herds of cattle and sheep increased in numbers. The soil became more and more alkaline in nature, two factors which contributed to the continual impoverishment of the land.

The fact is that the alkaline puszta with its short grass as known today is not the original natural landscape—it has been created by human activity. Why then have the three largest areas of the Hungarian Plain—Hortobágy, Apaj and Bugac—been nominated National Parks?

With the exception of the South Russian pusztas which are of natural origin, these areas are the only saliferous plains in Europe. In this lies their special attraction for Europeans. Here the flora and fauna have developed in harmony with the landscape and are known for their rarity throughout Europe. Here in the pools and low marshy areas of two Hungarian National Parks are the homes of birds unknown or rarely seen in the other parts of the continent. These reserves also provide a resting place and food for birds migrating from one continent to another. Equally interesting are the vestiges of the traditional life of the herdsmen who have for centuries been famous as breeders of cattle. Nationally and internationally there are good reasons for preserving these regions as National Parks equally attracting historians, sociologists and ecologists.

For Hungarians all the mystery and romance of these regions is summarized in the one word "puszta", a name we now share with all those who visit the eastern plains of Hungary.

12. The primeval juniper forest at Bugac is slowly recovering from the fires caused by human carelessness

13. The rambler rose is a favourite covering for farmsteads

14. The icy ribbon of the River Hortobágy in winter

15. Apaj, some 50 km south of Budapest, is the second largest puszta in Hungary, in the National Park of Kiskunság

16. Every year, in the last days of July, a fête is held to celebrate the local herdsmen and horsemen of Kiskunság. It is not only for tourists but also for the local people who want to preserve traditions. Some of the old herdsmen of Apaj also assemble for the same reason and often wear their traditional costumes, hats decorated with bustard feathers

As a schoolboy I was told that "when the Mongols devastated Cumania the Cuman king, Kuthen, fled with 40,000 families to Hungary where our king, Béla IV (1235–1270), settled them on the fertile lowlands of the Plain; the present inhabitants of Nagy- and Kiskunság being their descendants".

Later I marvelled that "the fertile lowlands of the Plain" were so uninhabited as to permit the settlement of 40,000 families.

The fact is that it was an inhospitable tract of sandy earth without roads and with very few inhabitants. The Cumans, being refugees, had no other choice: they had to settle where they were given a place.

István Györffy: Nagykunsági krónika
[Chronicle of the Nagykunság], 1922

17–22. The Kiskunság Fête for Herdsmen and Horsemen is one of the most attractive of the traditional festivities in Apajpuszta. The management of the National Park invites famous hat-makers, saddlers, knife-makers, furriers and potters to exhibit and offer for sale the finest products of their craft. Blue-dyers and gingerbread-makers are also at the fair.
There are numerous sporting events, including one round of the Hungarian coach-driving championship, an international jumping championship and several horse shows

23–26. We crouched hidden through the long, dark April night and the cool dawn to see the bustard cock displaying his feathers in the mating season.
There is national and international concern among conservationists to protect the great bustard. Approximately one hundred of the species have found refuge in Apajpuszta

27. Sand-storm in spring... >

The great bustard is a noble, heraldic bird and in the Hungarian Plain and in the meadowland of Transylvania it replaces the ostrich of the Southern hemisphere; it is even luckier than the latter because although bustards do not take off easily, when at last they are in the air, they fly well and steadily. In autumn they gather in flocks and in this way pass the winter. In old times herdsmen on their wild horses surrounded these flocks in freezing rain and drove them into some enclosure. This used to be the time of great fairs when the hats of young lads were ornate with many beautiful bustard feathers and even the landlords wore them proudly on their high caps.

Ottó Herman: A madarak hasznáról és káráról
[About Useful and Harmful Birds], 1901

28. The sand dunes in the district of Fülöpháza are unique in Europe inasmuch as they are still in permanent motion. In the region between the rivers Duna and Tisza people have been waging a struggle against the sand for centuries. In isolated farms it was at one time necessary to keep a shovel and spade overnight in the corner of the room, tools with which to prise open doors and windows blocked by the accumulation of sand blown by overnight gales.
In these moving sands it is very difficult for plants to strike root and there is little rain between spring and autumn. Yet these plants survive the summer heat and even blossom, as for instance the late maiden pink which has a coating of wax to reduce evaporation

29. The roots of the heath-rose and some of the dwarf shrubs strike roots deep into the soil, sometimes two metres deep. The roots of most plants that survive on sandy soil are much bigger than the visible parts

30. If an area of sandy soil which is sparsely covered with vegetation is disturbed for any reason, the surface is immediately reshaped into new and pleasingly undulating patterns

31. The leaves of the sand iris are protected against evaporation by a coating of wax

32. The blue globe-thistle is one of the prettiest and most frequently seen plants on the sand dunes in later summer

33. The motion of the sand is checked by varieties of moss and other ground-covering plants such as the sandbur which was brought here from North America

Here and there the sand is blown by the wind to create huge crested dunes, elsewhere it seems to flow gently like the waves of the sea; here and there a single poplar is buried so deep that only the topmost bough is visible, while others are scourged to the roots which claw the desert like long ropes or the legs of giant harvest-spiders. Here there is not a blade of grass, the only vegetation being a few brittle twigs of gorse. When there is no wind, all is silent… the desert comes alive with the wind as it rises from every direction, lifting clouds of sand high into the air where they colour it a faded yellow: then one can see nothing beyond ten paces.

Mór Jókai: Hétköznapok [Weekdays], 1846

34–38. The stone curlew, a rare and interesting bird of the sandy regions, chooses as its breading grounds quicksands, saline soils and areas periodically flooded by rivers. These birds find nesting places where the average number of sunny hours exceeds 2000 per year. Their nests are in reality small depressions generally scratched out by the hen in the soft soil with almost none of the usual nest-building materials, merely a few lumps of lime, one or two small pebbles and a few leaves or stems of plants.

There have been many contradictory observations concerning the development of the chicks. According to one observer, the young chicks walk away from the nest accompanied by their parents; according to others the parents fly away carrying the chicks in their beaks

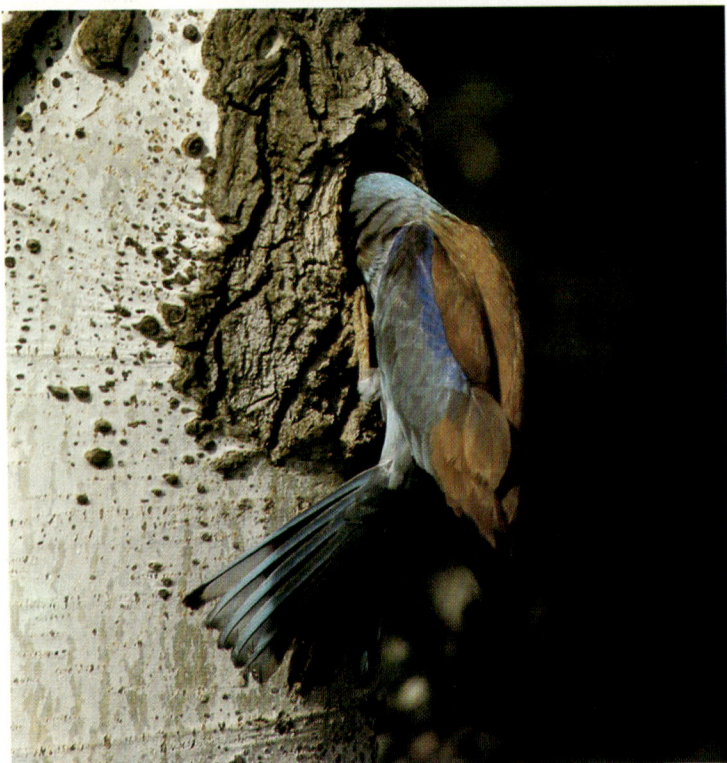

39–42. The rollers perched on a bough, "swinging" on the electric cables beside the road, or in flight, arrest the eye because of their brilliant blue colouring. Like the stone curlew, they thrive happily in the Kiskunság. The raise their young in hollows to which they return year after year. When bringing food for their young, rollers signal their approach with a special sound. We hear it from afar, at first faintly, then louder as it draws near. A sudden silence heralds our sight of the mother bird bending over the hollow, even disappearing inside to feed the chicks before scaring upwards to search for more food

43–44. Bugac has been one of the most popular areas of the National Park of Kiskunság since around 1930, when foreign tourists first began to take an interest in the puszta. The ancient tradition of cattle breeding lives on in this region and many features of the traditional costume of the herdsmen can still be seen. The varying brims of their high hats distinguish horse breeders from cow-herds, shepherds or swine-herds. Formerly they all wore black waistcoats with rows of silver buttons, wide white linen trousers and a white shirt. Sheepskin coats protected them from the cold, usually the shaggy black and white skins of the Hortobágy flocks, the tufts of which are 20–30 cm long. This hardy breed is well-adapted for survival in the severe winters of the Kiskunság puszta

… my salary for services rendered from St. Michael's Day to St. George's Day is 10 lambs from the spring lambing, 10 silver coins paid in instalments of two at the beginning of five consecutive months, then 15 bushels of wheat, 4 bushels of barley, 15 pounds of meat, 10 pounds of bacon, 5 pounds of salt, 1 bushel of mush, 1 pair of new boots and as much straw as can be placed on a two-oxen cart. Then I can keep through winter 25 sheep for myself, their feed being covered by the town. Then the milk, cheese and curd my master gives me is also mine. But once a week he must first hand in the part due to the town at the Puszta House. (1855)

Jolán Szappanos: A nagy pusztán [Life in the Puszta], 1981

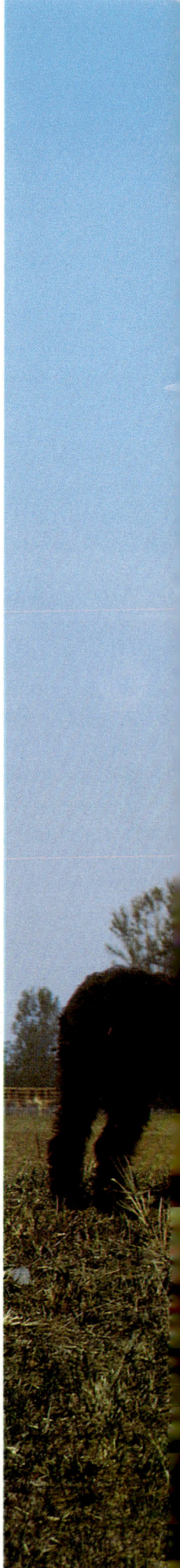

45–48. The Hungarian grey cattle, primarily draught animals but also providing excellent meat, were very popular in Europe in the Middle Ages. Enterprising traders drove the live-stock on foot to Vienna, Regensburg, Nuremberg, Munich, Ulm, Strasbourg, even Venice and further. The herdsmen's faithful companion is the dog, the black sheep-dog, called *puli*

49. Donkeys have few needs and were always a useful means of transport. Herdsmen liked them because they are clean animals who never wallow in dung

50. The long embroidered felt cloak, known as *szűr,* was expensive, every young peasant boy felt the need to buy one when he found a sweetheart. He would leave it, as if by accident, in her father's house. Then he had to watch anxiously, for if he saw it hanging outside the house, he knew that he had been rejected. The saying "to put out one's felt cloak" stems from this custom.
The coats were made of white or black-painted woollen cloth embroidered with coloured wool silk threads or appliqued with felt. Flower motifs—roses, tulips, lilies-of-the-valley—were usually chosen

51. A shepherd's crook is a working tool. He uses it in various ways: as a signal to his dog when turning the flock; for protection against man and beast; and as a support to lean on when he pauses for a moment's rest. Shepherds use the curved end of the crook for catching stray sheep by the leg

52. The corral is an enclousure where the herdsman can rest and store the wheelbarrow in which he kept food; this he would transport to the corral fixed to the end of a cart

53. In former times the herdsman had to stay near his beasts. The hipped hut, easily made, transported and erected, protected him in severe weather. It consisted of bundles of reeds bound tightly together with straw, a type of hut known in Hungary for centuries

54. A horseman of Bugac in the gala felt cloak of Kiskunság, standing by a corral in which dishes, clothing and tools were kept. Sometimes and extra section was added where horses could be tethered

I am Imre Bogár,
In the puszta live I,
In the land of Hung'ry,
Famous outlaw am I.

The Tisza it's murky
Has no mind to calm be,
Imre Bogár, famous Bogár
Wants to cross it quickly.

Wants to cross it quickly
Get some money quickly
At the fair of Kecskemét,
Wants to filch a pony.

Wants to filch a pony,
Sell it for good money,
At the fair of Szentmihály,
Wants to make some money.

Folksong

55. Resting

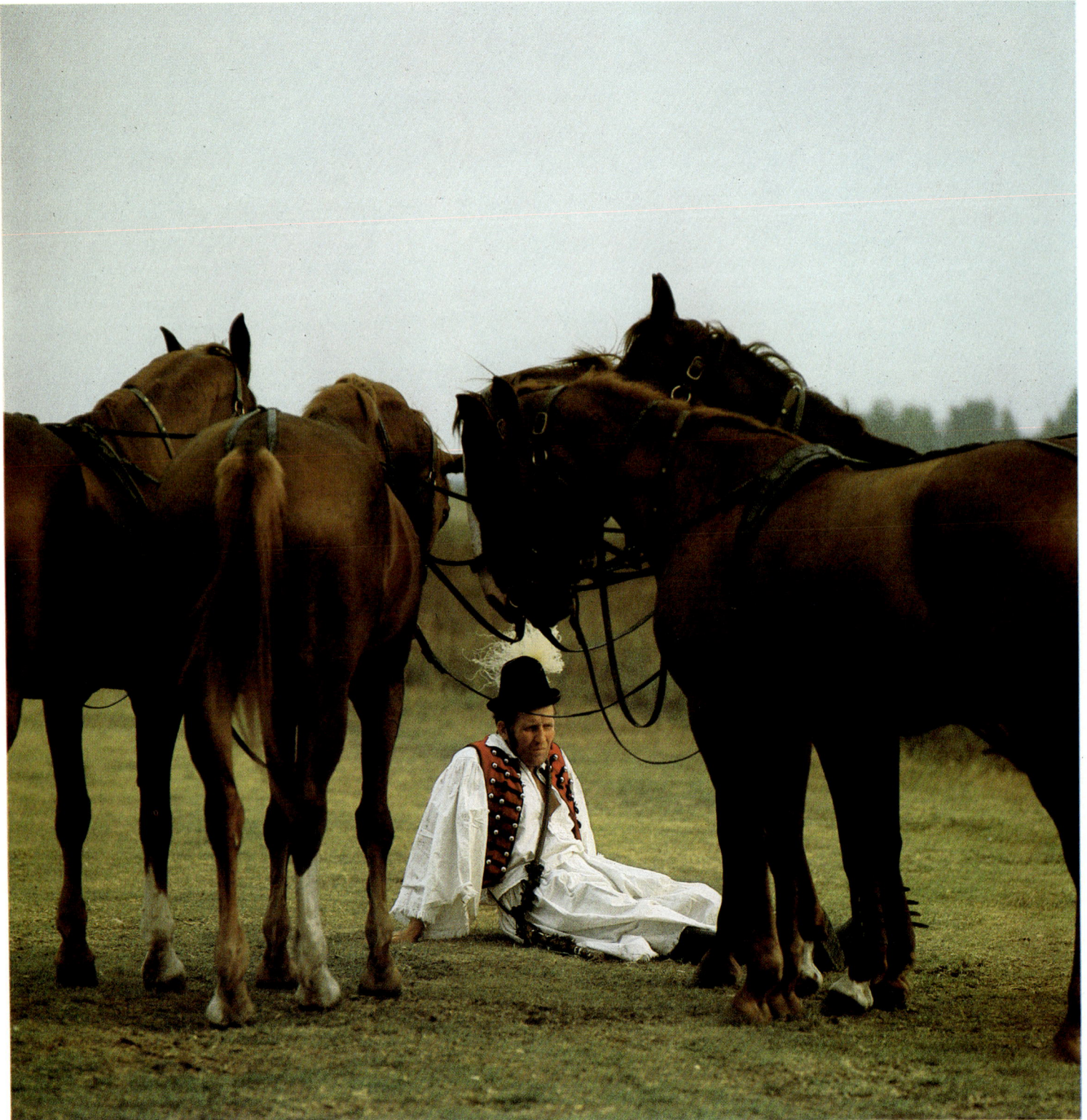

56–60. The horse show is one of the tourist attractions of Bugac: a team of five horses are driven at full speed, the horseman standing with one foot on each of the two rear horses. Such stunts are traditional, as a way of demonstrating the quality of the horses. They were also very useful skills for the highwaymen of the 18th and 19th centuries when trying to escape from the police—or desert from the army. They had to be able to make their horses lie down and remain motionless in the woods in response to a single swift command.

The herdsmen were good friends to the highwaymen, giving them food or showing them good hiding places. Some of them procured guns and became regular brigands, who, to the ordinary people, were good men who robbed the rich to pay the poor.

In the middle of the 19th century one of the most famous highwaymen of Kiskunság was Imre Bogár of Bugac, the hero of many legends and folk songs...

61–62. Ancient forests of juniper trees cover the greater part of Bugac, less dense than in previous centuries when the water level was much higher. Now clearings have been made for grazing, the sandy soil is instable, growth uncertain, but one still sees many varieties of juniper both young and old. The blue berries were used for dyeing, later for their perfume or bouquet as in the manufacture of Hollands (a type of gin)

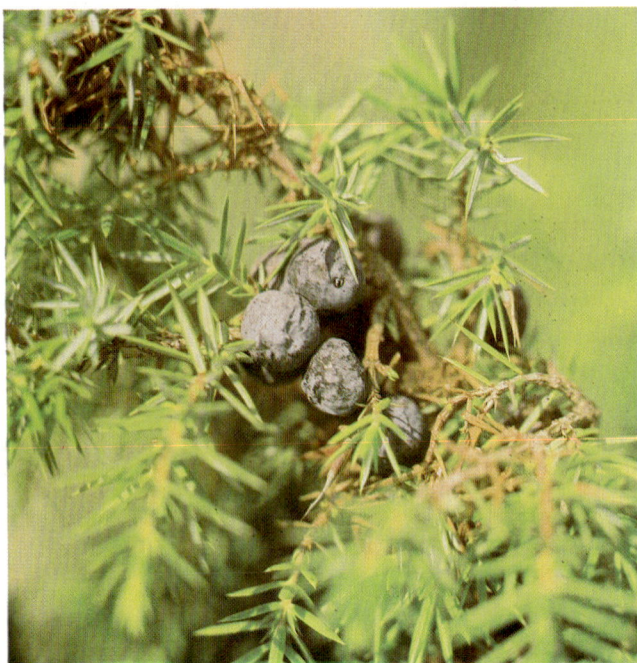

As time went on a means of dyeing was discovered —roots for red colouring, the wild crocus for saffron-yellow, and juniper berries for blue colouring. The juniper dye was used to make "blue-dyed" aprons in autumn from homespun calico. A hundred years ago the local people still knew a method of crushing juniper berries in aspen mortars and extracting the juice. This they heated in a cauldron over the glowing embers of a fire together with a certain quantity of pine-resin or "cat honey"—the resin found on blighted sour-cherry and apricot trees.

(Much later German factories bought the juniper berries of Bugac, train loads of them being exported for the manufacture of indigo-blue dyes for which there was a demand all over the world.)

Jolán Szappanos: A nagy pusztán [Life in the Puszta], 1981

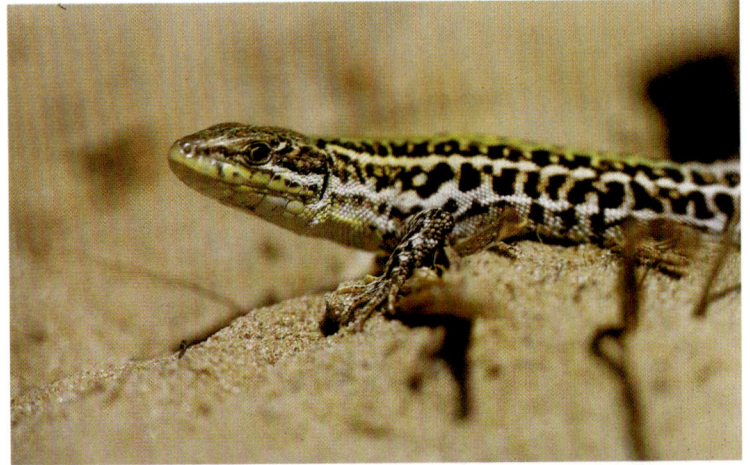

63. The ancient juniper forest of Bugac and the sand dunes of Kiskunság provide a home for many animals who live secretly, hidden from the eyes of men and only rarely to be seen as for instance the fast-moving Balkan wall lizard. It has never been found in Europe further west or north than here in Hungary. It needs even more heat than other types of lizard being mainly native to the hot mediterranean countries of South and South-East Europe

64. The pale violet blooms of the sand crocus herald the approach of autumn. This strange bulbous plant sprouts leaves and bears fruit in spring but it blossoms in autumn

65. On the low ground on both sides of the bridge leading to the Herdman's Museum at Bugac there are marsh-loving plants, one of being the most beautiful of the protected species, the gentian

66. The habitat of the orsinis viper is strictly protected – underground holes in the Great Forest of Bugac. It is less dangerous than is commonly believed. There is a possible danger if bitten, but it is a timid creature, rarely seen, for it is sensitive to the smallest sound and retreats at the first warning of danger. There are few of these vipers and their number is diminishing

67. One is also lucky to see the wild rabbits who live among the dunes. They emerge from their subterranean tunnels below the soft sandy earth only at dusk to look for food. They move warily and if disturbed flee in zig-zag tracks back to the safety of the tunnels

68. The more inaccessible parts of the Great Forest of Bugac provide a home for a diminishing number of predatory birds. The hawk builds its nest in the upper tiers of the great trees, often 10–15 metres above the ground

69. Within the low valleys of Fülöpháza, Fülöpszállás and Szabadszállás we can see a succession of saline lakes like a string of pearls. Their names have much etymological interest.
The salt content of these lakes is high, and though they cover an extensive area they are very shallow and in dry weather there can be total evaporation

70. Around these ponds people used to fish mainly for themselves but also for the market. The old fish-baskets sometimes seen in farmyards are a relic of this extinct trade

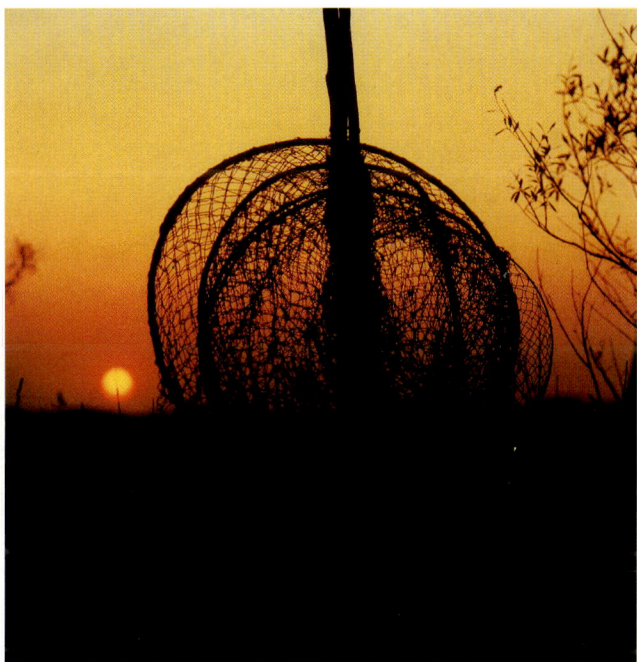

… In the Spring, mirror-like pools of still water reflect the rays of the sun: at the first sheep-shearing these pools provided water for drinking and washing. But in the dog days they used to dry out. The women rejoiced, swept up and gathered into sacks the sodium carbonate deposited at the bottom of the pools and took it to the towns for sale. In those days it was used everywhere for scouring and scrubbing. For the women it was a profitable business—a free gift from the puszta.

Jolán Szappanos: A nagy pusztán [Life in the Puszta], 1981

71. Vegetation is scarce on the flat banks and islands of these saline lakes of Kiskunság but it can support the colonies of birds which arrive yearly. Some of these birds are not found elsewhere in Central Europe. The illustrated text of the notice erected at the lake-side is as follows: "This is our empire, we build our nests and raise our young here. Please do not disturb!"
One of the finest specimens of the tern, the sea swallow, also builds its nest here. The male brings fish to the hen not only in the courting period but also when she sits on the eggs

72. The avocet is not especially timid but it always shows great caution when coming near to a nest full of eggs. Sometimes it pretends to have an injured wing and so lures any dangerous humans or animals to a safe distance

... In marshy regions [the black-winged stilt] can still be seen in Hungary but unfortunately less frequently now as the ponds and fens are gradually drying out.

... This is a sad loss to us for the black-winged stilt is one of the delights of the swamps, conspicuously beautiful whether we see it prancing daintily over the grassless sandy shore or wading knee-high in shallow water near the banks, nodding from time to time, and finally, in slow flight, with its long legs stretched backwards. It is rather like a very small stork although its way of life and movements are quite different, and it is of a quite different species.

István Chernel: Magyarország madarai [The Birds of Hungary], 1899

73–76. The black-winged stilt is one of the rarest birds of the
saline lakes. It likes to build its nest on small hillocks rising
from the water and on floating plants gathered by the wind to
form a raft. It is amusing to watch it settling on the nest,
bending itself this way and that as it arranges its
disproportionately long red legs like some giant grasshopper.
The number of these birds varies from year to year;
sometimes none are to be seen in Hungary, another year there
may be only one or two pairs. In recent years they have turned
up unexpectedly in the region beyond the Tisza and the plains
of Hortobágy on the alkaline waters abandoned by ducks

In Hungary the black-headed gull has completely adapted itself to farming, and where its flocks have settled in the lake-land areas the black-headed gull is a very loyal follower of the plough, and the most industrious destroyer of everything which damages layland, meadow-land and grassland. It never ceases to pick up insects, worms and every creature which is considered harmful in farming: it feeds its young with them so that where the black-headed gull has its colonies, agriculture does not complain of damage done by noxious insects.

Ottó Herman: A madarak hasznáról és káráról
[About Useful and Harmful Birds], 1901

77. The shrill cries of black-headed gulls are heard everywhere in early spring. By the end of March they have often completed their nests and occupy every available place on the islands of the alkaline lakes. There can be as many as several thousand birds on one island

78. The lake-side at dusk

79. The Lake of Kolon in Izsák has luckily survived several attempts to drain it, and is still a treasured habitat of marsh-loving plants

80. Walking round the deserted pools, swamps and reed banks of the Hungarian Plain we begin to realise that this region provided an asylum for survivors of successive invasions by the Mongols and Turks. To survive they had to know their way through the treacherous swamps: a similar knowledge of the area is still necessary for contemporary travellers

The Cumans had no thought for draining the inland waters. Left to them, the land would have remained uncultivated. For 600 years they accepted a watery landscape and now they feel as fish cast on the shore. Their herds have disappeared, and with them the unique characteristics of their race. Within the space of a few decades the land has been drained, the meadows and fens replaced by saline quicksands which extend further year by year. This soil does not tolerate the plough! It waits for the return of the floods, the herdsmen, the wild horses! The mirage lurks on the horizon, still faintly visible, as if hoping to float its deceptive vapours over the Cuman land once again.

István Györffy: *Nagykunsági krónika*
[Chronicle of the Nagykunság], 1922

81. Among the reeds and young willows beside the Lake of Kolon herons hatch their young. Every species of heron known in Hungary, including the night heron, is represented here

82–83. The European pond turtle breeds where the lakes have sandy shores. The female lays her eggs in a hole dug by herself and buries them carefully in the sand. The heat of the sun hatches them. The little turtles emerge at the end of August or early in September, and instantly march into the nearest water

84. In spring the shallow water near the edge of the lake is covered by a soft layer of broad-leafed wool sedge

85. Fishing has always been popular among Hungarians

86. In the golden age of fishing loaches were caught together with dogfish, a small fish native only to the Carpathian Basin and the marshes of the Plain

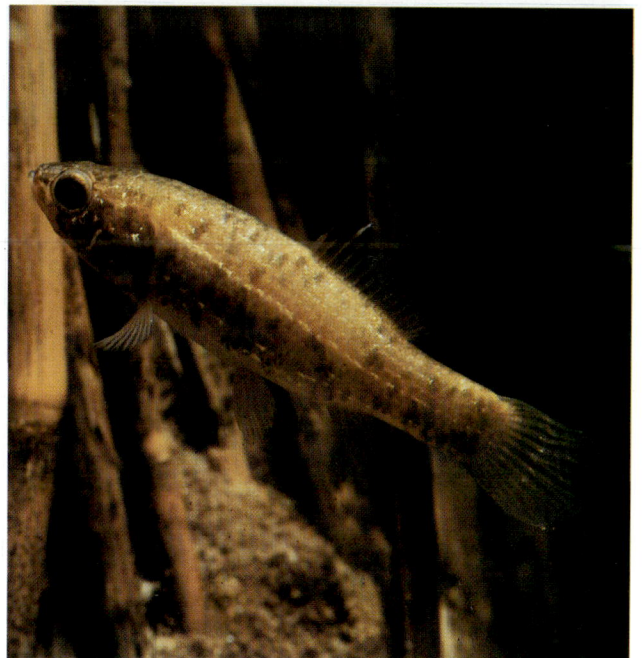

87. The marshes by the Lake of Kolon are the home of many animals and the habitat of rare plants. Of the 22,000 orchid species known throughout the world over 40 species exist in Hungary. Fifteen species can be found in the National Park of Kiskunság, and nine by the Lake of Kolon. The military orchid can be seen, but it is extremely rare

88. The bee-orchid not only resembles a bee but also produces a perfume to attract insects

89. The most common Hungarian orchid is the marsh orchid

90. Thanks to increased protection the snow-white great heron—the emblem of Hungarian nature conservation—is to be seen in ever-growing numbers

... The great white heron is truly the finest bird of the fens and marshes, and with the proudest stance, a ruler among the masses. The sight of these slender creatures, slim and dazzling white, as they alight on the green, flowering meadows is indeed splendid. Their feathers glisten in the sunshine like new-fallen virgin snow; with their veil-like aigrettes they remind us of young girls in their bridal gowns.

... In flight too they are beautiful, like silken veils driven by the wind. As they fly over the green sea of reeds we hear their intermittent 'craw-craw'. They are seen as brilliant white against the cloudy sky into which they seem to dissolve and disappear.

...As if fearful for its feathers, the great white heron, more than other birds of the species, avoids man who hunts it specifically for this decorative feature. Aigrettes are much sought after as the most desirable ornament for the Hungarian headdress. To Hungarians the bird represented nobility, pride and refinement, its fine feathers were unsuitable for the clothes of simple people and were only to be seen worn by royalty and later by members of the aristocracy.

István Chernel: Magyarország madarai [The Birds of Hungary], 1899

91–92. In the National Park of Kiskunság there is a nature reserve and an exhibition of aspects of local life in the region past and present. Characteristic farmsteads of the past have also been restored

93–97. It was 100–120 years ago that farmers began to leave the villages and live permanently in isolated farmsteads on the land they cultivated so that they could give more attention to their crops and animals. These farmsteads were not independent settlements, they belonged to a town or village. As the years went by the larger settlements could no longer support these ever-growing families.

Maps dating from the late 1700s indicate approximately 1000 detached farms around Kecskemét. By the middle of the 19th century there remained 177.

Self-reliance was the ambition of those who chose to live in these isolated farmsteads. Each family tried to produce everything they needed: therefore they had their own cattle for meat, milk, and transport. Sometimes, though rarely, one can still find draught-cattle at work.

The farming community lived in close relationship with the natural environment. The stork nesting on the chimney of their thatched roofs was a welcome guest

98–101. In the past three decades the countryman's life has changed substantially. First he was not allowed to build new farmsteads, nor was he allowed to make use of the national electricity supply, nor even to extend his roads. Gradually the more isolated families moved into the villages where conditions were more favourable, and their children moved still further to work in factories. There remained the older generation, but their children built new houses in the village.

It was easier to retain a roadside farmstead and these remained for some time. In the 1960s and 1970s it was permissible to make use of the national electricity supply, and although the owners might change, the farmsteads remained. Those few who obstinately remained in the isolated farmsteads battled against the inevitable. Their lives were hard indeed and when death claimed them, their farmsteads fell into ruins. Now the very foundations are overgrown

He lived and died among the poor, he respected God, paid his taxes, outlined tulips on sheepskin-coats with coloured cotton threads, planted vines and raised children. When Death came to gather him he fell to dust in the vineyards of the Lord, leaving no trace in the manner of all peasants.

... In the halls of time there is no echo of his steps; indeed he preferred to walk barefoot, and had no ambition to be recorded in history, nor did history consider it necessary to do so, and was equally neglectful of his like.

Ferenc Móra: *Az édesapám vétke [The Sin of My Father],* 1928

Oh, beloved mother,
Our beloved mother, she is gone.
Oh, how you suffered!
For two years we tried to cure you in vain, without avail,
Oh, how the Good Lord did make you suffer!
Oh, you are at rest now.
Dear brothers, gather round,
Mourn our dear departed mother!
Oh, she lived seventy-four years,
Oh, she was so good to us,
She granted all our wishes, every one.
She brought us up.
Now they're taking her away.
Father dear, you are alone now,
But we will stay, we will not desert you.
May God bless you, our beloved mother!
In the earth's belly may you find solace!
May divine brightness be your lot.

Lament collected by Tekla Dömötör at Szerep in 1964

102. Dusk in the puszta of Kiskunság

103–106. The wooden crosses and headboards in the old
cemetery of Ócsa are all in the traditional style. Scholars differ
as to their origin: some trace them back to the ancient Cuman
headboards of the pagan era, others find in them the influence
of the Turks

107. This water-lily, golden yellow, beautifies slow-moving backwaters

108. This backwater of the Tisza with its wooded banks was created by regulation work undertaken in the middle of the 19th century. There is still occasional flooding, and therefore the vegetation of the tide-lands is unchanged

Loveliest of all places is Szikra, on the banks of the Tisza, a fertile hilly region cultivated from time immemorial. Today there are neither summer-houses nor rest houses but the time will come when visitors will still admire the panorama from the gorse-strewn hillside washed by the pale waters of the Tisza as it meanders between the willows.

László Bagi jun.: Kecskemét múltja és jelene [The Past and Present of Kecskemét], 1896

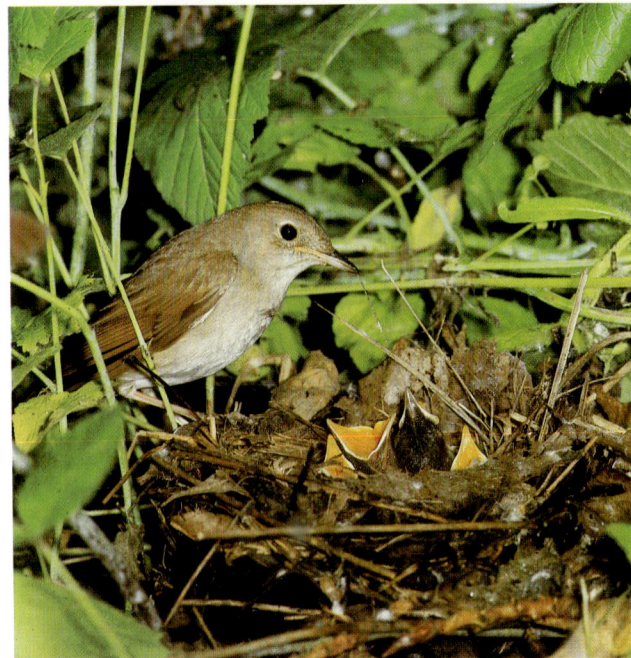

109. The red-backed shrike hoards for future use both insects and reptiles by pinning them on thorns and prickles

110. In the middle layers of the forest foliage, about six metres above the ground, the great spotted woodpecker raises its young in the hollow of a branch

111. The nightingale, renowned for the beauty of its song, makes its nest, well-hidden, in dense undergrowth. When it is very hot, the nightingale must give water to the young ones and refresh their feathers

112. The spotted flycatcher has settled in the hollow of a tree-trunk

113–114. Many birds find food and shelter in the luxuriant undergrowth of the willow-groves and tiered woods bordering the backwater of the Tisza

115. The Tisza >

116. On the Hortobágy plain there is no barrier between us and the far horizon; where the puszta meets the sky we see the faint outlines of farms, barns and draw-wells

117. The inn at Hortobágy was built in the early nineteenth century. Inns were sited so that travellers could cover the intervening distance between meals. They provided for travellers, cattle-drivers and local herdsmen. The Hungarian name for these inns, "csárda", first occurs in a document dated 1662. Since 1773 they have also been described as "rest-houses of the puszta"

What is the puszta of Hortobágy?

An unknown island within the confines of the known world…

This "island" is surrounded by the everyday world of crowded towns, well-cultivated fertile fields with farm-steads, tobacco plantations, young forests and gardens; but the soil of the puszta has never been broken by the plough. I can rightly call it "unknown" for even those who, attracted by its fame, travel to the borders of the puszta, rarely continue further than the inn at Hortobágy. Visitors to the twice-yearly cattle sales also find no occasion to go beyond the cattle-rings set up by the bridge on the banks of the Hortobágy. It is rare indeed for anyone to penetrate the vast spaces of the puszta itself, and without a competent guide it is as well that they do not make the attempt. The puszta is the domain of no more than 260 herdsmen, three veterinaries, the commissar of the puszta and the local magistrates.

Mór Jókai: Napraforgók [Sunflowers], 1891

118. The spring migration of cranes and the sound of their cooing is a reminder that these birds once built their nests in the swamps of the Plain

119. The water-birds have found new homes in the reeds, beside artificial fish-ponds and on the islands

120. The tools and tackle of fishermen, now obsolete

121. Springtime floods on the puszta remind us of floods in the past when people had to escape in rowing boats

Flood waters covered the plains of the Hortobágy: The Tisza had burst its banks at Füred and Nánás; the River Hortobágy was rising, the ponds enlarging of the puszta where only the tops of the bulrushes and reeds were now visible, and the inn at Hortobágy, like a half-collapsed Niniveh, was isolated in a sea of mud. God's soul walked on the virgin waters; dead cattle, stray rafts, fragmented haystacks and the garbage from flooded streets floated over a watery plain on which the enraged breeze had scattered showers of broken reeds.

Lajos Kuthy: Hazai rejtelmek [Domestic Mysteries], 1846

122–124. As a result of irrigation work and dams completed in the 19th century only the deepest marshes of the Hortobágy have survived. Summer geese hide their nests in these few remaining natural waters, also among the reeds of artificial fish-ponds. The herdsmen call them blonde geese because of their light feathers

The poet's song is wafted through the air.
Wild geese pass overhead.
In spring the Hortobágy provides the most extensive resting-place for geese known throughout the world. They fly to these pastures from the North and here they fall victim to the sportsmen lying in wait, hour after hour, hidden in ditches, careless of snow and rain, watching patiently for their prey. I am not a hunter and my heart aches for those free-flying birds; better that I were the target. But in spring sportsmen swarm about the inn, counting the wild geese they could have bought for a fraction of the price of a gun.

The song written in the sky is mine.

The geese swim in the blue-white milky waters and cry out their messages, ecstatic and jubilant. They feel the warmth of the sun, the freshness of the air, they fly apart and come together in pairs... Spring is here, it is the mating season and soon the loneliness of caring for the young ones.

Into the velvet softness of the sky they imprint their cries of joy and woe.

Zsigmond Móricz: A Hortobágy tavaszi lélegzete
[Spring in the Hortobágy], 1942

125. The spoonbills arrive early in spring. They are related to storks rather than herons; they fly with necks outstretched whereas herons draw in their necks. They are named spoonbills because their beaks widen at the tip like spoons. The upper mandible of their beaks was used by fishermen as tablespoons

126. Purple herons break the reeds for nest-building on the shores of open waters: standing on the broken reeds they watch their food with infinite patience without moving

127. The whiskered tern likes to build its large nest on the leaves of the white water-lily. The base consists of reed stems arranged like spokes of a wheel. As the nests float on open water the wind often damages them, sometimes simply sweeping them off the leaves

128–129. In the most treacherous boggy parts of the larger marshes and among reeds the rare white-winged black tern makes its nest. This is the most westerly point in Europe where it nests.
Unlike others of the species, the white-winged black tern starts hatching after having laid the first egg. Until three eggs have been laid the hen protects the nest and warms the eggs, the male bringing her food

130–131. The centre of Hungarian cattle-breeding has always been the Plain. In the National Park of Kiskunság and Hortobágy bones of sheep dating from the Migration Period have been excavated; but relics of the black and white Hungarian sheep with its "V"-shaped horn date only from the sixteenth and seventeenth centuries. It is difficult to know whether this particular breed was introduced from the South during the Turkish occupation or whether it was the result of local breeding. Certainly there is a real possibility that the black-and-white sheep of Hortobágy were bred here by Hungarians from the finest stock brought here by the first settlers

... The sheep-shearers have come. The sheep have already been washed on the previous day where the River Hortobágy has been dammed for the purpose. Now they are driven into barns where the women shear off their luxuriant coats with sharp scissors. There is one barn for the noble merinos, another for the native Hungarian sheep, some black, some white, their heads rather goat-like, and with the twisted and tilted horns of a wild beast.

If some naïve visitor should venture to ask how sheep (rams and ewes) develop those tortuous horns the shepherd might say that every day he presses a hot loaf of bread over the sheep's horns and twists them... he looks so very serious that it would be offensive to doubt him.

Mór Jókai: Napraforgók [Sunflowers], 1891

132. Necessity has been the best teacher known to shepherds. They even found a use for sheep dung. By stamping on it they shaped it into square blocks which they dried in the sun for winter fuel and to heat their large earthenware ovens. They also used these blocks of dung as bricks to build kennels for their dogs *(komondors)*.

A few komondors were capable of driving off wolves. Some scholars say that the name is of Cuman origin with the meaning "dog of Cumans"

133. The *kuvasz* helps the herdsman to protect his flock

In the kingdom of the Hortobágy shepherds were ranked lowest. Herdsmen and horse-trainers were the aristocrats of the region and swineherds might be described as squireens. But shepherds, though discounted because there were so many, were not to be belittled. The proud sign burned by the sun of the free puszta on the open faces of Hungarian herdsmen shone also on the brow of shepherds. For him there was none of the humiliation sometimes suffered by domestic servants. He walked with head high, lord and master of his own domain. They were as experienced and knowledgable as many a herdsman or horse-trainer, the aristocrats of the puszta, who rode about the plain. Some shepherds were like lonely poplars in the puszta, famed for their skill far beyond the plains of the Hortobágy…

Pál Móricz: Hortobágyi legendák [Legends of the Hortobágy], 1927

134. Herdsmen's costumes were more traditional than anything worn by peasants. They insisted on the old-fashioned distinctive garments which set them apart from others. Nowadays their clothes combine the old and the new, but the tools of their trade, for instance the shepherd's crook, are still made in the traditional style

136. Herdsmen in general, but shepherds in particular, were skilled in the craft of leather-dressing, their knowledge handed down through the generations so that they were able to make their own clothes and simple articles for their own use

135, 137. The coarse wool of the black-and-white sheep was not fit for industrial use; in the 18th century sheep with finer wool were introduced into Hungary. The stock registered in Debrecen in 1880 consisted of 58,311 sheep with fine wool and only 4,055 Hortobágy sheep. Now there are also many merino sheep in the Hortobágy

138–139. It was long believed that the grey Hungarian cattle were brought here by Hungarians when they first occupied the Carpathian Basin. More recently bones have been excavated indicating that this breed of cattle was probably introduced by the Cumans, but it is possible that they were also bred here in Hungary during the period when the aurochs were diminishing in numbers and Christians were not allowed to eat horse meat. It is at any rate certain that before the natural flow of the Tisza was controlled to prevent flooding the Hortobágy region was eminently suitable for the old style of cattle-breeding. The moist soil near the river produced a plentiful supply of grass for fodder. Hungarian grey cattle thrived on the swampy pastures and the hot summer sunshine, and could survive a scarcity of food in winter

>140–143. These dark bulls are the lords of the puszta. There is a story that among the herd of Junoshát one unruly bull attacked the cattle-herd who had to send for assistance, fearing that the bull would soon take his own place as cattle-head. In August the bulls from different points of the puszta are driven together into one large bull-herd. They fight among themselves for precedence and the earth shakes beneath their hoofs... The weak avoid the attentions of the strong, and the struggle between equals has to be stopped by the herdsmen with the help of their dogs. They must be separated before they begin to injure each other

144. The dry alkaline puszta seems smooth as a table from afar but at close quarters one can see that the earth has been baked hard by the combined effect of wind, rain and sun, then cracked into mosaic-like segments, some of them slightly higher than others. Here the Kentish plover makes its nest, a small bird known to herdsmen as the "salt-loving, rolling, whistling bird"

145. A Hortobágy sub-species of the short-toed lark is the only bird which is native to Hungary

146. The camomile blooms everywhere. Outside the strictly protected areas it is still gathered for medicinal purposes; a long-handled, fine-toothed rake is used

147. The Transylvanian plantain, established since time immemorial, is now a protected plant

148–149. Pratincoles enjoy the heat of the sun when they arrive in Hungary in late April or early May. They lay their three eggs in a little depression scooped out of the bleak alkaline soil with a few stalks of artemisia or on pats of dried cattle-dung. The young have protective colouring so that they can hide, unseen by human eye, in the hollow footprints of an animal or in a crack in the earth

150. The lowest plateau of the puszta is the so-called "blind" alkaline level covered by a white saline deposit when the pools left by spring rains have evaporated. Here grows the camphor, a flower which turns purple in the autumn

151. By the end of summer the saline pastures are enlivened by the violet colouring of the salt flower

... The parts of the puszta covered by native soda are bleak and poverty-stricken. Owing to its physical and chemical particularities this is one of the worst soils. It is lumpy and close-textured so that fluids cannot circulate throught it, nor does it permit the air to penetrate; plants cannot root themselves in this soil; and every element necessary for the growth of plants is missing. The pastures are of the poorest quality and the roads impassable. As the last puddles dry out one can see angular clay prisms, smooth-surfaced, separated by cracks into which one can insert two fingers and more than a span in depth. Although the upper surface of these prisms is hard and dried out, the base is still soft so that without due care carts and beasts might easily sink deep into the ground and rescue would be very difficult.

Lajos Zoltai: A Hortobágy [The Hortobágy], 1911

152–153. Red-footed falcons catch their prey in flight, not with their beaks but with their claws. They catch water-beetles, peck off their hard wing-cases and eat them as they fly or bring them to their young. Their hunting ground is the open puszta where they hang or hide on tufts of vegetation watching the insects

154. About ten days before taking flight the young stand on the edge of the nest and study the world about them

155. The forest of Ohat is the last vestige of the ancient oak forests of the puszta

156–162. The first record of the stud farm of Hortobágy is dated 1671. This provides interesting information about the Nonius breed which was originally bred in France. During the Napoleonic wars it was taken as booty by the Austrian cavalry and later was acquired for the stud-farm at Mezőhegyes. It was first known in Debrecen in 1873 when the town introduced the Nonius breed onto the puszta owned at that time by Debrecen. The puszta, where there is regular racing, provides the necessary conditions for training horses with the stamina needed for contemporary racing and other sports

163–165. The horsemen of the puszta, like the cowherds and shepherds, still wear, with few adaptations, the traditional costume of their calling. Horse breeders wear wide blue linen trousers reaching to their boot-tops, blue shirts with wide sleeves and a waistcoat. The cattle-herdsmen wear a similar costume of white linen. Hats are made of felt by traditional craftsmen. The inhabitants of the puszta generally make many of their own tools as well.

The long whips used by riders and herdsmen are very decorative, the whip carefully woven, the handle bound with leather to prevent slipping: the handle is carved in patterns like those on the shepherd's crook

166. In the latter part of the 19th century there was some building on the plains. These houses for herdsmen and shelters for animals have not usually survived as they were made mainly of reeds or adobe. The characteristic kitchen of Hortobágy herdsmen is the so-called "flat-iron" which consists of sheaves of reeds placed one beside the other in the shape of a flat iron but leaving a small aperture at the top. This protective wall of reeds prevents even the strongest wind from extinguishing the fire under the cauldron

167. Stud-farm on the Hortobágy

168. Hungary's longest stone bridge, with nine arches, was built at Hortobágy between 1827 and 1833. We know from records that this was already an important meeting point in the 13th century but spring floods made it difficult to cross the Hortobágy river. The wooden bridge, erected in the 14th century, was several times repaired and reinforced before the building of the present stone bridge

169. The inn at Hortobágy, built in traditional folk style is near the bridge. In 1699 an inn of sorts was built on this site by the ancient highway leading to Pest-Buda, and one of the innkeepers' tasks was to collect duty

The Inkeeper's Accounts at Hortobágy: Lajos Fésüs

Fixed prices: Soup 20 fillérs, beef with broth 60, vegetable with meat 60, roast beef with potatoes 90, stewed beef or mutton 60, roast or stewed pig 90, fish 80, scrambled eggs (three eggs) 50, one lightly-boiled egg 18, boiled or baked pasta 50, a glass of beer 20, one litre of table wine 80, of mulled wine 120, of mountain wine 100. A pre-ordered lunch with soup, meat, vegetables, pasta, bread, 2 crowns 40 fillérs. Groups arriving on foot are advised to announce their arrival one day in advance.

Transport fees: two horse carriage 10 crowns for one day. For half-days and shorter journeys price to be agreed on in advance.

Digging of hunter's ditch: 2 crowns. Filling up: 1 crown.

Lajos Zoltai: A Hortobágy [The Hortobágy], 1911

Fairs are a long-established tradition in the puszta of Hortobágy. They were at one time known as "travelling" or "highwayman"-fairs. They were held yearly, starting always on the morning of the first Wednesday after Whitsun. Dealers used to come to the Hortobágy from every part of the country and in fact the real business began on Monday.

This highwayman-fair was a gala occasion for herdsmen. A few of them stayed to guard the cattle while everyone else put on their holiday clothes, and celebrated with wine, music and dancing. The inn resounded to the noise of their laughter and sometimes there were harsh words between old enemies who even came to blows.

Pál Móricz: Hortobágyi legendák [Legends of the Hortobágy], 1927

170–177. The stone bridge is the centre of the Hortobágy "bridge fair" held yearly in August. It was first held in 1825 near the inn when the wooden bridge was still in existence.
Fairs lasted for three days. The livestock market was held on Wednesday and Friday, and the country fair lasted until Sunday evening or Monday noon. The cattle brought high prices, but there were also small everyday items for sale

178. The reeds in the autumn sunshine of early evening

179. October mist

180–182. As the mists clear the wild geese arrive. The small ringed plovers arrive in small groups in early October. The large plovers predominate among the Hortobágy geese: their characteristic call and their V-shaped migration flights are well known; they arrive in the second half of October and gather in November.

We no longer see clouds of geese consisting of thousands of birds: their way of life and their living conditions have changed.

Now the wild-geese of Hortobágy live as if by routine—they take to the air at down, return in search of food, drink wherever they find still water and return to their roosting places. This entails the second group flight of the day. They arrange themselves in dense groups in the middle of the water and receive newcomers with loud cackling. As the sun disappears behind the clouds the wild geese prepare to fly into their chosen places in the gathering dusk. In autumn the puszta is one large roosting-place for birds

183. The silence of the puszta in winter ... only the grey cattle walk in the fresh snow...>

The round disc of the sun is still visible but now it gives no warmth. Clouds gather leaving only a narrow band of blue sky above the horizon. Above and below the sun, like pale reflections of itself, two more discs of subdued light begin to float among the clouds. Slowly they fade and a gentle drizzle of rain begins to fall... at first slowly, then more heavily, shrouding the earth in mist.

It swallows the lonely towers of distant villages, the trees clustered round farm-steads and finally the cattle-pens, the herdsmen's shelters and the high arms of the wells are all lost in the mist. The herd itself is gathered into the all-enveloping obscurity. Now the herdsman is alone, alone in a God-made universe.

Péter Veres: Falusi krónika [Rural Chronicle], 1941

184. Winter dawn >>

There is an old saying in Debrecen that those who
have not yet seen the Hortobágy deserve twenty-five strokes
but those who go to see it, deserve fifty!
My own visits to the puszta are countless; so too
the number of strokes I deserve. But I do not count the cost.
I have travelled along the unmarked roads of the
Hortobágy by coach and by car. I have waded in
rubber boots through the swamps and slept in small huts
curtained with cobwebs and I have slept there under the stars.
Why do I feel this passion for the Hungarian puszta?
No words can express what I know in my heart.

Title of the Hungarian original: A magyar puszta. Kiskunság, Hortobágy
Corvina Kiadó, Budapest, 1987
Translated by Éva Polgár
Translation revised by Elizabeth West
Design by: István Murányi

ISBN 963 13 2528 8
Printed in Hungary, 1987
Kner Printing House, Békéscsaba